Text © 2013 by Sally Muir and Joanna Osborne
Photographs © 2013 by Diana Miller

While every effort is made to ensure the safety and comfort of the animals who might use the projects in this book, the authors and publisher cannot accept responsibility for any illness or accident arising from the use of these projects.

The material was previously published in the book *Pet Projects: The Animal Knits Bible* (ISBN 978-1-60085-127-8) first published in 2007 by Quadrille Publishing Limited, Alhambra House, 27-31 Charing Cross Road, London, WC2H 0LS

First published in this format 2013

The Taunton Press
Inspiration for hands-on living®

The Taunton Press, Inc., 63 South Main Street, PO Box 5506, Newtown, CT 06470-5506
e-mail: tp@taunton.com

Cover Design: Kimberly Adis
Interior Design: © 2007 Quadrille Publishing Limited
Photographer: Diana Miller

Library of Congress Cataloging-in-Publication Data
Muir, Sally.
 Dog coats & collars : patterns to knit for pampered pets / Sally Muir and Joanna Osborne.
   pages cm
  ISBN 978-1-62710-098-4 (pbk.)
1. Knitting--Patterns. 2. Dogs--Equipment and supplies. I. Osborne, Joanna. II. Title. III. Title: Dog coats and collars.
 TT825.M783 2013
 746.43'2--dc23
Printed in the United States of America
10 9 8 7 6 5 4 3 2 1

Table of Contents

DOG COATS

We have designed a range of coats to suit your dog's every whim. The Soccer Coat will give your dog a sense of purpose when playing with a ball. In an equally manly vein, there is the simple, timelessly elegant Cable Coat. One of our most practical garments, it has a masculine Sean Connery feel combined with contemporary retro chic. As we all know, spots never go out of fashion, and any dog wearing the Britart-inspired Spot Dog Coat will feel equally at home in Central Park or the backyard. Finally, ravishing yet practical, the Floral Dog Coat is for the dog who wants to stand out from the crowd. For an extravagant occasion, team it with the Floral Party Dog Collar on page 16.

SOCCER **DOG** COAT

LEVEL
Intermediate

SIZES
See page 32 for dog measurements and sizes.

FINISHED COAT MEASUREMENTS

	Width of coat	Length to neck shaping
Extra small	14in/35.5cm	12in/30.5cm
Small	15³⁄4in/40cm	14in/35.5cm
Medium	18¹⁄2in/47cm	18in/45.5cm
Large	24in/61cm	22in/55.5cm
Extra large	26¹⁄2in/67cm	24in/61cm

MATERIALS
Light/DK Weight Yarn (CYCA 3) *approx. 260 yds (260: 390: 520: 650)
in main color* **MC** (Shown in *Jaeger Matchmaker Merino DK*)
Approx. 130 yds of same yarn in a contrasting color **A**
Pair of size 3 (3.25mm) knitting needles
Pair of size 6 (4mm) knitting needles
Set of four size 3 (3.25mm) double-pointed knitting needles

GAUGE
22 sts and 30 rows to 4in/10cm measured over St st using size 6 (4mm) needles.

ABBREVIATIONS
See page 31.

CHART NOTE
The charts (p. 30) are worked in St st. When working from the charts, read odd-numbered rows (k rows) from right to left, and even-numbered rows (p rows) from left to right.
When working the chart patterns, use the intarsia method, knitting with a separate small ball (or long length) of yarn for each area of color and twisting yarns together on wrong side when changing color to avoid holes.

TOP OF COAT
With size 3 (3.25mm) needles and MC, cast on 42 (46: 56: 76: 86) sts.
1st rib row (RS) *K1, p1; rep from * to end.
(Last row is repeated to form k1, p1 rib patt.)
Work 3 rows more in rib, ending with a WS row.
Change to A and work 2 rows more in rib.
Break off A.
Cont with MC only, work 4 rows more in rib.
Change to size 6 (4mm) needles.
Beg St st with rib borders as follows:
Next row (RS) [K1, p1] twice, k into front and back of next st, k to last 5 sts, k into front and back of next st, [k1, p1] twice.
Next row Rib 4 sts as set, p to last 4 sts, rib 4 sts as set.
Rep last 2 rows 7 (9: 9: 11: 11) times, ending with a WS row.
(58 (66: 76: 100: 110) sts.)

Extra Small and Small only
Cont in St st only, set position of number chart (see page 30) as follows:
Next row (RS) K27 (31: -: -: -)MC, k5A, k26 (30: -: -: -)MC.
Next row P24 (28: -: -: -)MC, p10A, p24 (28: -: -: -)MC.

Medium, Large, and Extra Large only

Work even as set, with St st at center and 4-st rib border along each side edge, until work measures - (-: 5½: 7: 8)in/ - (-: 14: 17.5: 20)cm from cast-on edge (measuring up center of panel), ending with a WS row. Set position of number chart (see page 30) as follows:

Next row (RS) Rib 4 sts in MC, k- (-: 32: 44: 49)MC, k5A, k- (-: 31: 43: 48)MC, rib 4 sts in MC.

Next row Rib 4 sts in MC, p- (-: 29: 41: 46)MC, p10A, p- (-: 29: 41: 46)MC, rib 4 sts in MC.

Cont foll chart as set and working 4-st rib borders until work measures - (-: 6: 8: 9)in/ - (-: 15: 20: 22.5)cm from cast-on edge, ending with a WS row.

All sizes

Beg with a k row, work all sts in St st and cont foll chart until all 40 chart rows have been completed (then cont with MC only) **and at the same time** cont in patt as now set until work measures 5½ (7 :11: 13: 14)in/14 (17.5: 28: 33: 35.5)cm from cast-on edge, ending with a p row.

(**Note:** If required, increase or reduce length of coat here and match this change on gusset.)

Mark for leg openings

Mark each end of last row with a colored thread to indicate beg of leg openings.

Cont in St st until work measures 8 (10: 14: 16 : 17½)in/20 (25.5: 35.5: 40.5: 44.5)cm from cast-on edge, ending with a p row.

Mark each end of last row with a colored thread to indicate end of leg openings.

Cont in St st until work measures 10 (12: 16: 18: 20)in/25.5 (30.5: 40.5: 45.5: 50.5)cm, ending with a p row.

Next row (RS) K8 (10: 12: 18: 20), k2tog, k to last 10 (12: 14: 20: 22) sts, k2tog, k8 (10: 12: 18: 20).

Purl 1 row.

Rep last 2 rows row 5 (7: 8: 14: 14) times. (46 (50: 58: 70: 80) sts.)

Work even in St st until work measures 12 (14: 18: 22: 24)in/30.5 (35.5: 45.5: 55.5: 61)cm from cast-on edge, ending with a p row.

Break off yarn and leave sts on a st holder.

GUSSET

With size 3 (3.25mm) needles and MC, cast on 16 (22: 28: 34: 38) sts.

Work 4 rows in k1, p1 rib as for top of coat.

Change to A and work 2 rows more in rib.

Break off A.

Cont with MC only, work 2 rows more in rib.

Change to size 6 (4mm) needles.

Beg with a k row, work in St st until gusset measures 3½ (3: 5: 5: 5)in/6.5 (7.5: 13: 13: 13)cm from cast-on edge, ending with a p row.

Mark for leg openings

Mark each end of last row with a colored thread to indicate beg of leg openings.

Cont in St st throughout, work until leg openings measure same as leg openings on top of coat, ending with a p row.

Mark each end of last row with a colored thread to indicate end of leg openings.

Work until gusset measures 6 (7: 9: 10: 12)in/15 (17.5: 22.5: 25: 30.5)cm from cast-on edge, ending with a p row.

Set position of badge chart (see page 30) as follows:

Next row (RS) K7 (10: 13: 16: 18)MC, k1A, k8 (11: 14: 17: 19)MC.

Next row P7 (10: 13: 16: 18)MC, p3A, p6 (9: 12: 15: 17)MC.

Cont in St st foll chart as set until chart row 20 has been completed (then cont with MC only) **and at the same time** cont as set until work measures 8 (8½: 10½: 10: 12)in/20 (21.5: 26.5: 25: 30.5)cm from cast-on edge, ending with a p row.

Dec 1 st at each end of next 4 (6: 9: 11: 12) rows, ending with a p (p: k: k: p) row. (8 (10: 10: 12: 14) sts.)

Work even until gusset measures 9 (10: 12: 14: 15)in/23 (25.5: 30.5: 35.5: 38.5)cm from cast-on edge, ending with a p row.

Break off yarn and leave first 4 (5: 5: 6: 7) sts on one st holder and rem 4 (5: 5: 6: 7) sts on another st holder.

TO FINISH

Press top of coat and gusset lightly on wrong side, following instructions on yarn label and avoiding ribbing.

With right sides together and matching leg-opening markers, sew gusset to top of coat, leaving seam open between markers for front-leg openings.

Turn coat right side out.

Collar

The collar is worked so that it is divided at the center front (under the chin) after 4 rows in rib.

With RS facing and using set of four size 3 (3.25mm) double-pointed needles and A, k 4 (5: 5: 6: 7) sts from left gusset st holder, k 46 (50: 58: 70: 80) sts from top-of-coat st holder and k 4 (5: 5: 6: 7) sts from right gusset st holder (distributing sts evenly on 3 needles and knitting with 4th needle). (54 (60: 68: 82: 94) sts.)

Work 4 rounds in k1, p1 rib, ending at center front.

Now turn work and start working collar back and forth in rows of garter st (knit every row) so that it is divided at center front as follows:

Next row (RS of collar) K13 (15: 17: 20: 23), k into front and back of next st, k to last 14 (16: 18: 21: 24) sts, k into front and back of next st, k13 (15: 17: 20: 23).

Next row (WS of collar) K to end.

Rep last 2 rows 7 times, ending with a WS row.

Change to MC and knit 2 rows.

Break off MC.

Change to A and knit 4 rows.

Bind off knitwise.

Edging on front leg openings

With RS facing and using set of four size 3 (3.25mm) double-pointed needles and A, pick up and knit 30 (38: 38: 46: 46) sts around one front leg opening.

Work 6 rounds in k1, p1 rib.

Change to MC and work 1 round more in rib.

Break off MC.

Change to A and work 2 rounds more in rib.

Bind off loosely in rib.

Work second edging in same way.

CABLE **DOG** COAT

LEVEL
Easy

SIZES
See page 32 for dog measurements and sizes.

FINISHED COAT MEASUREMENTS
	Width of coat	Length to neck shaping
Extra small	12¼in/31cm	12in/30.5cm
Small	14¾in/37.5cm	14in/35.5cm
Medium	17¾in/45cm	18in/45.5cm
Large	23in/58.5cm	22in/55.5cm
Extra large	25½in/65cm	24in/61cm

MATERIALS
Light/DK Weight Yarn (CYCA 3) approx. 260 yds (260: 260: 390: 520) in color of your choice (shown in *Rowan Felted Tweed*)
Pair of size 3 (3.25mm) knitting needles
Pair of size 6 (4mm) knitting needles
Short double-pointed size 6 (4mm) knitting needle or cable needle

GAUGE
22 sts and 30 rows to 4in/10cm measured over St st using size 6 (4mm) needles.
14-stitch cable panel measures approximately 1½in/4cm wide.

ABBREVIATIONS
C10B = slip next 5 sts onto cable needle and hold at back of work, k5, then k5 from cable needle.
Also see page 31.

TOP OF COAT
With size 3 (3.25mm) needles, cast on 42 (46: 56: 76: 86) sts.
1st rib row *K1, p1; rep from * to end. (Last row is repeated to form k1, p1 rib patt.)
Work 5 rows more in rib.
Change to size 6 (4mm) needles.
Beg cable patt as follows:
1st patt row (RS) [K1, p1] twice, k into front and back of next st, k9 (11: 16: 26: 31); for cable panel, work p2, k10, p2; k9 (11: 16: 26: 31), k into front and back of next st, [k1, p1] twice.
(44 (48: 58: 78: 88) sts.)

2nd patt row [K1, p1] twice, p11 (13: 18: 28: 33); for cable panel, work k2, p10, k2; p11 (13: 18: 28: 33), [k1, p1] twice.
3rd patt row [K1, p1] twice, k into front and back of next st, k10 (12: 17: 27: 32); for cable panel, work p2, k10, p2; k10 (12: 17: 27: 32), k into front and back of next st, [k1, p1] twice.
(46 (50: 60: 80: 90) sts.)
4th patt row [K1, p1] twice, p12 (14: 19: 29: 34); for cable panel, work k2, p10, k2; p12 (14: 19: 29: 34), [k1, p1] twice.
5th patt row [K1, p1] twice, k into front and back of next st, k11 (13: 18: 28:

33); for cable panel, work p2, k10, p2; k11 (13: 18: 28: 33), k into front and back of next st, [k1, p1] twice.
(48 (52: 62: 82: 92) sts.)
6th patt row [K1, p1] twice, p13 (15: 20: 30: 35); for cable panel, work k2, p10, k2; p13 (15: 20: 30: 35), [k1, p1] twice.
7th patt row [K1, p1] twice, k into front and back of next st, k12 (14: 19: 29: 34); for cable panel, work p2, C10B, p2; k12 (14: 19: 29: 34), k into front and back of next st, [k1, p1] twice.
(50 (54: 64: 84: 94) sts.)
This sets patt with St st at each side of a

central 14-st cable panel and a 4-st rib border along each side edge.

Cont in patt as set, crossing cable (as in 7th patt row) on every foll 10th row, **and at the same time** cont to inc 1 st at each end (inside rib borders) of 4 (6: 6: 8: 8) foll alt rows (RS rows), ending with a RS row. (*58 (66: 76: 100: 110) sts.*)

Work even in patt as set until cable panel measures 3 (4: 6: 8: 9)in/7.5 (10: 15: 20: 22.5)cm from cast-on edge, ending with a WS row.

Next row (RS) K22 (26: 31: 43: 48); work next 14 sts in cable panel patt as set; k22 (26: 31: 43: 48).

Next row P22 (26: 31: 43: 48); work next 14 sts in cable panel patt as set; p22 (26: 31: 43: 48).

This sets patt with St st at each side of central 14-st cable panel.

Cont in patt as now set until cable panel measures 5$\frac{1}{2}$ (7: 11: 13: 14)in/ 14 (17.5: 28: 33: 35.5)cm from cast-on edge, ending with a WS row.

(**Note:** If required, increase or reduce length of coat here and match this change on gusset.)

Mark for leg openings
Mark each end of last row with a colored thread to indicate beg of leg openings.
Cont in patt until cable panel measures 8 (10: 14: 16: 17$\frac{1}{2}$)in/20 (25.5: 35.5: 40.5: 44.5)cm from cast-on edge, ending with a WS row.
Mark each end of last row with a colored thread to indicate end of leg openings.
Cont in patt until cable panel measures 10 (12: 16: 18: 20)in/25.5 (30.5: 40.5: 45.5: 50.5)cm from cast-on edge, ending with a WS row.

Next row (RS) K8 (10: 12: 18: 20), k2tog, k12 (14: 17: 23: 26); work next 14 sts in cable panel patt as set; k12 (14: 17: 23: 26), k2tog, k8 (10: 12: 18: 20). (*56 (64: 74: 98: 108) sts.*)

Next row P21 (25: 30: 42: 47); work next 14 sts in cable panel patt as set; p21 (25: 30: 42: 47).

Next row K8 (10: 12: 18: 20), k2tog, k11 (13: 16: 22: 25); work next 14 sts in cable panel patt as set; k11 (13: 16: 22: 25), k2tog, k8 (10: 12: 18: 20). (*54 (62: 72: 96: 106) sts.*)

Working in patt as set, cont to dec 1 st at each end of 4 (6: 7: 13: 13) foll alt rows (RS rows), ending with a RS row. (*46 (50: 58: 70: 80) sts.*)

Work even in patt until cable panel measures 12 (14: 18: 22: 24)in/ 30.5 (35.5: 45.5: 55.5: 61)cm from cast-on edge, ending with a WS row.
Break off yarn and leave sts on a st holder.

GUSSET

With size 3 (3.25mm) needles, cast on 16 (22: 28: 34: 38) sts.
Work 6 rows in k1, p1 rib as for top of coat.
Change to size 6 (4mm) needles.
Beg with a k row, work in St st until gusset measures 3$\frac{1}{2}$ (3: 5: 5: 5)in/6.5 (7.5: 13: 13: 13)cm from cast-on edge, ending with a p row.

Mark for leg openings
Mark each end of last row with a colored thread to indicate beg of leg openings.
Cont in St st throughout, work until leg openings measure same as leg openings on top of coat, ending with a p row.
Mark each end of last row with a colored thread to indicate end of leg openings.
Work until gusset measures 8 (8$\frac{1}{2}$: 10$\frac{1}{2}$: 10: 12)in/20 (21.5: 26.5: 25.5: 30.5)cm from cast-on edge, ending with a p row.
Dec 1 st at each end of next 4 (6: 9: 11: 12) rows, ending with a p (p: k: k: p) row. (*8 (10: 10: 12: 14) sts.*)
Work even until gusset measures 9 (10: 12: 14: 15)in/23 (25.5: 30.5: 35.5: 38.5)cm from cast-on edge, ending with a p row.
Do not break off yarn and leave sts on a st holder.

TO FINISH

Press top of coat and gusset lightly on wrong side, following instructions on yarn label and avoiding cable panel.
With right sides together and matching leg-opening markers, sew right side edge of top of coat to left side edge of gusset, leaving seam open between markers for front-leg openings.

Turtleneck collar
With RS facing and size 3 (3.25mm) needles, k 8 (10: 10: 12: 14) sts from gusset st holder and k 46 (50: 58: 70: 80) sts from top-of-coat st holder. (*54 (60: 68: 82: 94) sts.*)
Work these sts in k1, p1 rib until collar measures 4 (4: 5: 6: 6)in/10 (10: 12.5: 15: 15)cm.
Bind off loosely in rib.
With right sides together, sew remaining side seam as for first side seam, and sew collar seam reversing seam on last 2 (2: 2$\frac{1}{2}$: 3: 3)in/5 (5: 6.5: 7.5: 7.5) cm of collar for turnback.

FLORAL **DOG** COAT

LEVEL
Difficult

SIZES
See page 32 for dog measurements and sizes.

FINISHED COAT MEASUREMENTS

	Width of coat	Length to neck shaping
Extra small	10in/25.5cm	10in/25cm
Small	14in/35.5cm	13in/33cm
Medium	15½in/39cm	16in/40.5cm
Large	17in/43cm	20in/50.5cm
Extra large	19¾in/50cm	22in/56cm

MATERIALS
Light/DK Weight Yarn (CYCA 3) approx. 260 yds (260: 260: 390: 520)
(shown in *Jaeger Matchmaker Merino DK*) in main color **MC**, for background
Approx. 130 yds of same yarn in each of 4 different colors—**A**, **B**, **C**, and **D**—
for motifs
Pair of size 3 (3.25mm) knitting needles
Pair of size 6 (4mm) knitting needles
4 (5: 5: 5: 5) buttons

GAUGE
22 sts and 30 rows to 4in/10cm measured over St st using size 6
(4mm) needles.

ABBREVIATIONS
See page 31.

CHART NOTE
The chart (p. 26) is worked in St st. When
working from the chart, read odd-numbered
rows (k rows) from right to left, and even-
numbered rows (p rows) from left to right.
When working the chart pattern, use the
intarsia method, knitting with a separate
small ball (or long length) of yarn for each
area of color and twisting yarns together
on wrong side when changing color to
avoid holes.
Note: The chart shows only the St st section
of the coat; the seed stitch borders are not
included on the chart.

TO MAKE COAT
With size 3 (3.25mm) needles and MC,
cast on 42 (64: 72: 80: 96) sts.
Work border in seed st as follows:
1st row (RS) *K1, p1; rep from * to end.
2nd row P1, k1; rep from * to end.
3rd row [K1, p1] twice, k into front and
back of next st, *p1, k1; rep from * to last
7 sts, p1, k into front and back of
next st, [p1, k1] twice, p1.
(44 (66: 74: 82: 98) sts.)
4th row [P1, k1] 3 times, k next st (the inc
st), p1, k1; rep from * to last 7 sts, p1, k
next st (the inc st), [k1, p1] twice, k1.

5th row [K1, p1] twice, k into front and
back of next st, *k1, p1; rep from * to last
7 sts, k into front and back of next
st, [k1, p1] 3 times.
(46 (68: 76: 84: 100) sts.)
6th row Rep 2nd row.
Change to size 6 (4mm) needles.
Cont to shape coat, beg St st patt with
seed st side borders as follows:
1st patt row (RS) K1, [p1, k1] twice
for seed st border; k into front and back
of next st, k to last 6 sts, k into front and
back of next st; p1, [k1, p1] twice for seed
st border.

2nd patt row P1, [k1, p1] twice for seed st border; p to last 5 sts; k1, [p1, k1] twice for seed st border.
3rd and 4th patt rows Rep 1st and 2nd patt rows. *(50 (72: 80: 88: 104) sts.)*
Set position of chart patt (see pages 26–27) on next 2 rows (chart rows 5 and 6) as follows:
5th patt row (RS) Using MC seed st 5 sts; using MC k into front and back of next st, k27 (38: 42: 46: 54)MC, k4A, k7 (18: 22: 26: 34)MC, using MC k into front and back of next st; using MC seed st 5 sts. *(52 (74: 82: 90: 106) sts.)*
6th patt row Using MC seed st 5 sts; p3 (14: 18: 22: 30)MC, p3A, p2MC, p6A, using MC p to last 5 sts; seed st 5 sts.
Cont foll chart as set and working 5-st seed st borders **and at the same time** cont to inc 1 st at each end (inside seed st borders) of 2 foll alt rows (RS rows), ending with a RS row.
(56 (78: 86: 94: 110) sts.)
Work even in patt as set (when chart patt has been completed, cont using MC only) until coat measures 10 (13: 16: 20: 22) in/25 (33: 40.5: 50.5: 56)cm from cast-on edge, ending with a WS row.
(**Note:** If you need to lengthen coat to fit your dog, work some extra rows here before starting neck shaping.)

Shape neck
Next row (RS) Work 23 (34: 36: 38: 44) sts in patt, then turn, leaving rem sts on a st holder.
Working on these sts only, cont as follows:
**Keeping patt correct throughout, dec 1 st at neck edge of next 3 rows.
Dec 1 st at neck edge of 4 (4: 4: 2: 4) foll alt rows.
Dec 1 st at neck edge of every 4th row 1 (1: 1: 2: 1) times.

(15 (26: 28: 31: 36) sts.)
Work even until coat measures 13 (17: 21: 26: 29)in/33 (43: 53: 66: 73.5)cm from cast-on edge, ending with a WS row.

Change to size 3 (3.25mm) needles and MC only.**
Work 2 rows in seed st, ending with a WS row.

Small, Medium, Large, and Extra Large only
Next row (buttonhole row) (RS) Seed st - (3: 5: 8: 13) sts, [work 2tog, yo, seed st 7 sts] twice, work 2tog, yo, seed st 3 sts.

Extra Small only
Next row (buttonhole row) (RS) Seed st 1 st, work 2tog, yo, seed st 7 sts, work 2tog, yo, seed st 3 sts.

All sizes
Work 3 rows in seed st.
Bind off.
With RS facing, return to rem sts, slip center 10 (10: 14: 18: 22) sts onto a st holder, rejoin yarn and work in patt to end.
Work as for first side of neck from ** to **.
Work 6 rows in seed st.
Bind off.

STRAP
With size 3 (3.25mm) needles and MC, cast on 13 sts.
1st row *K1, p1; rep from * to last st, k1.
(Last row is repeated to form seed st.)
Work in seed st until strap measures 2 (4½: 6: 9½: 11)in/5 (11: 15: 24: 28)cm from cast-on edge.
Next row (buttonhole row) Seed st 5 sts, work 2tog, yo, seed st 6 sts.
Work in seed st until strap measures 3 (5½: 7: 10½: 12)in/7.5 (14: 17.5:

26.5: 30.5)cm from cast-on edge.
Rep buttonhole row.
Work in seed st until strap measures 4 (6½: 8: 11½: 13)in/10 (16.5: 20.5: 29: 33)cm from cast-on edge.
Rep buttonhole row.
Work in seed st until strap measures 5 (7½: 9: 12: 14)in/12.5 (19: 22.5: 30.5: 35.5)cm from cast-on edge.
Bind off.

TO FINISH
Block and press coat lightly on wrong side, following instructions on yarn label and avoiding seed st borders. Do not press strap.

Neck edging
With RS facing, size 3 (3.25mm) needles and MC, pick up and knit 22 (28: 32: 36: 40) sts along right neck edge (picking up first 5 sts along edge of seed st border), knit 10 (10: 14: 18: 22) sts from center neck st holder, pick up and knit 22 (28: 32: 36: 40) sts up left neck edge. *(54 (66: 78: 90: 102) sts.)*
Work 2 rows in seed st, ending with a RS row.
Next row (buttonhole row) (WS) Seed st to last 4 sts, yo, work 2tog, seed st 2 sts (buttonhole should be in line with other buttonholes).
Work 2 rows more in seed st.
Bind off.
Sew 3 (4: 4: 4: 4) buttons to front opening border to correspond with buttonholes.
Sew strap to right side-edge of coat 5½ (8: 10½: 13: 15)in/14 (20.5: 26.5: 33:5: 38)cm from cast-on edge.
Sew button for strap to wrong side of left side-edge of coat to correspond with position of strap.

PARTY **DOG** COLLARS

Dress up your dog for a special occasion in a party dog collar. The covers are slipped onto the dog's collar and then popped over its head. There are five designs to choose from: a majestic ruffle, a chic tapestry of flowers, dashing spots, a Hell's Angel collar for the rottweiler in your dog, or perhaps a seductive garland of flowers.

RUFFLE **DOG** COLLAR

LEVEL
Easy

SIZES
The finished collar cover measures approximately 1¹/₂in/4cm wide for all sizes, and the lengths are as follows:
Extra-extra small—to fit collar size 10in/25cm
Extra small—to fit collar size 12in/30.5cm
Small—to fit collar size 14in/35.5cm
Medium—to fit collar size 16in/40.5cm
Large—to fit collar size 18in/45.5cm
Extra large—to fit collar size 20in/50.5cm

MATERIALS
Fingering/Super Fine Weight Yarn (CYCA 1) approx. 200 yds. (200: 400: 400: 400: 400) in main color **MC** (shown in *Jaeger Matchmaker Merino 4-Ply*)
Lace Weight Yarn approx. 229 yds in a contrasting color **A** (shown in *Rowan Kidsilk Haze*)
Pair of size 3 (3.25mm) knitting needles

GAUGE
28 sts and 36 rows to 4in/10cm measured over St st using size 3 (3.25mm) needles and MC.

ABBREVIATIONS
See page 31.

TO MAKE COLLAR COVER
With size 3 (3.25mm) needles and MC, cast on 24 sts.
Work 2 rows in garter st (knit every row).
Beg St st section as follows:
1st row (RS) K6, p1, k17.
2nd row P17, k1, p6.
Rep last 2 rows until collar cover measures 9 (11: 13: 15: 17: 19)in/22.5 (28: 33: 38: 43: 48)cm from cast-on edge, ending with a WS row.
Work 2 rows in garter st, ending with a WS row.
Next row (RS) Bind off first 12 sts knitwise, k to end. *(12 sts.)*
Work 10 rows in garter st.
Bind off knitwise.

RUFFLE
With size 3 (3.25mm) needles and A, cast on 165 (195: 231: 267: 306: 363) sts.
Work 2 rows in garter st (knit every row).
Break off A, change to MC, and cont as follows:
Work 12 rows in garter st.
Next row *K3tog; rep from * to end. *(55 (65: 77: 89: 102: 121) sts.)*
Work 2 rows in garter st.
Next row [K1, p1, k1] all into each st to end (to inc twice into each st).
(165 (195: 231: 267: 306: 363) sts.)
Work 12 rows in garter st.
Break off MC, change to A, and cont as follows:

Work 2 rows in garter st.
Bind off knitwise.

TO FINISH
Press collar cover lightly on wrong side, following instructions on yarn label.
With wrong side of ruffle facing right side of collar cover, sew ruffle to collar cover, stitching along center of ruffle and through line of rev St st on collar cover.
Fold collar cover in half lengthwise and sew long side edges together to form a tube.
Sew bound-off edge of collar cover to corresponding section of cast-on edge.
Slip cover onto dog's collar, positioning buckle over garter st section.

FLORAL **DOG** COLLAR

LEVEL
Intermediate

SIZES
The finished collar cover measures approximately 4cm/1¹/₂in wide for all sizes, and the lengths are as follows:
Extra small—to fit collar size 12in/30.5cm
Small—to fit collar size 14in/35.5cm
Medium—to fit collar size 16in/40.5cm
Large—to fit collar size 18in/45.5cm
Extra large—to fit collar size 20in/50.5cm

MATERIALS
Fingering/Super Fine Weight Yarn (CYCA 1) approx. 200 yds in main color **MC**, for background (shown in *Jaeger Matchmaker Merino 4-Ply*)
Small amount of same yarn in **A** (light blue/Dewberry), for flower petal motifs
Small amount of same yarn in each of **B** (blue-green/Sea Green 006), **C** (lavender/Lavender 005), and **D** (green/Apple 015), for leaf motifs and flower centers (shown in *Rowan Scottish Tweed 4-Ply*)
Pair of size 3 (3.25mm) knitting needles

GAUGE
28 sts and 36 rows to 4in/10cm measured over St st using size 3 (3.25mm) needles and MC.
31 rows to 4in/10cm measured over chart patt using size 3 (3.25mm) needles.

ABBREVIATIONS
See page 31.

CHART NOTE
The chart (p. 29) is worked in St st. When working from the chart, read odd-numbered rows (k rows) from right to left, and even-numbered rows (p rows) from left to right. When working the chart pattern, use the intarsia method (see page 14), knitting with a separate small ball (or long length) of yarn for each area of color and twisting yarns together on wrong side when changing color to avoid holes.

TO MAKE COLLAR COVER
With size 3 (3.25mm) needles and MC, cast on 24 sts.

Work 2 rows in garter st (knit every row).
Beg with a k row, work 0 (2: 10: 20: 28) rows in St st, ending with a WS row.
Beg with a k row and chart row 1, work in St st foll chart (see page 29) until all 98 chart rows have been completed, ending with a p row.
Using MC only and cont in St st, work 0 (2: 10: 20: 28 rows), ending with a p row—collar cover measures 11 (13: 15: 17: 19)in/28 (33: 38: 43: 48)cm from cast-on edge.
Work 2 rows in garter stitch, ending with a WS row.
Next row (RS) Bind off first 12 sts knitwise,

k to end. *(12 sts.)*
Work 10 rows in garter st.
Bind off knitwise.

TO FINISH
Block and press lightly on wrong side, following instructions on yarn label.
Fold collar cover in half lengthwise with right sides together and sew long side edges together to form a tube. Turn right side out and press again.
Sew bound-off edge of collar cover to corresponding section of cast-on edge.
Slip cover onto dog's collar, positioning buckle over garter st section.

SPOT **DOG** COLLAR

LEVEL
Easy

SIZES
The finished collar cover measures approximately 1¹/₂in/4cm wide for all sizes, and the lengths are as follows:

Extra-extra small—to fit collar size 10in/25cm
Extra small—to fit collar size 12in/30.5cm
Small—to fit collar size 14in/35.5cm
Medium—to fit collar size 16in/40.5cm
Large—to fit collar size 18in/45.5cm
Extra large—to fit collar size 20in/50.5cm

MATERIALS
Fingering/Super Fine Weight Yarn (CYCA 1) approx. 200 yds in main color **MC,** for background (shown in *Jaeger Matchmaker Merino 4-Ply*)
Small amount of same yarn in each of 5 (5: 5: 5: 5: 6) contrasting colors, for spot motifs
Pair of size 3 (3.25mm) knitting needles

GAUGE
28 sts and 36 rows to 4in/10cm measured over St st using size 3 (3.25mm) needles and MC.

ABBREVIATIONS
See page 31.

CHART NOTE
The chart (p. 29) is worked in St st. When working from the chart, read odd-numbered rows (k rows) from right to left, and even-numbered rows (p rows) from left to right. When working the chart pattern, use the intarsia method, knitting with a separate small ball (or long length) of yarn for each area of color and twisting yarns together on wrong side when changing color to avoid holes.

TO MAKE COLLAR COVER
With size 3 (3.25mm) needles and MC, cast on 24 sts.
Work 2 rows in garter st (knit every row).

Beg with a k row, work 4 rows in St st, ending with a p row.
Beg with a k row and chart row 1, work in St st foll chart (see page 29) until all 16 chart rows have been completed, using desired contrasting color for first spot motif.
Cont as set, repeating chart rows 1–16 and using desired random contrasting colors for spot motifs, until collar cover measures approximately 9 (11: 13: 15: 17: 19)in/22.5 (28: 33: 38: 43: 48)cm from cast-on edge and ending with a chart row 8 (a p row).
Cont with MC only, work 2 rows in garter st, ending with a WS row.

Next row (RS) Bind off first 12 sts knitwise, k to end. *(12 sts.)*
Work 10 rows in garter st.
Bind off knitwise.

TO FINISH
Block and press lightly on wrong side, following instructions on yarn label.
Fold collar cover in half lengthwise with right sides together and sew long side edges together to form a tube. Turn right side out and press again.
Sew bound-off edge of collar cover to corresponding section of cast-on edge.
Slip cover onto dog's collar, positioning buckle over garter st section.

HELL'S ANGEL **DOG** COLLAR

LEVEL
Intermediate

SIZES
The finished collar cover measures approximately 1¹/₂in/4cm wide for all sizes, and the lengths are as follows:
Small—to fit collar size 14in/35.5cm
Medium—to fit collar size 16in/40.5cm
Large—to fit collar size 18in/45.5cm
Extra large—to fit collar size 20in/50.5cm

MATERIALS
Fingering/Super Fine Weight Yarn (CYCA 1) approx. 191 yds in main color **MC** (black) for background (shown in Rowan *4-Ply Soft*)
Small amount of same yarn in **A** (gold), for lettering and part of motif (shown in Twilley's *Gold Fingering*)
Small amount of same yarn in each of **B** (white) and **C** (red) (shown in Rowan *4-Ply Soft*), for motifs
Pair of size 3 (3.25mm) knitting needles

GAUGE
28 sts and 36 rows to 4in/10cm measured over St st using size 3 (3.25mm) needles and MC.

ABBREVIATIONS
See page 31.

CHART NOTE
The chart (p. 29) is worked in St st. When working from the chart, read odd-numbered rows (k rows) from right to left, and even-numbered rows (p rows) from left to right. When working the chart pattern, use the intarsia method, knitting with a separate small ball (or long length) of yarn for each area of color and twisting yarns together on wrong side when changing color to avoid holes.

TO MAKE COLLAR COVER
With size 3 (3.25mm) needles and MC, cast on 24 sts.

Work 2 rows in garter st (knit every row). Beg with a k row, work 2 (8: 16: 26) rows in St st, ending with a p row.
Beg with a k row and chart row 1, work in St st foll chart (see page 29) until all 106 chart rows have been completed, ending with a p row.
Using MC only and cont in St st, work until collar cover measures 13 (15: 17: 19)in/ 33 (38: 43: 48)cm from cast-on edge, ending with a p row.
Work 2 rows in garter stitch, ending with a WS row.
Next row (RS) Bind off first 12 sts knitwise, k to end. *(12 sts.)*

Work 10 rows in garter st.
Bind off knitwise.

TO FINISH
Block and press lightly on wrong side, following instructions on yarn label.
Fold collar cover in half lengthwise with right sides together and sew long side edges together to form a tube. Turn right side out and press again.
Sew bound-off edge of collar cover to corresponding section of cast-on edge.
Slip cover onto dog's collar, positioning buckle over garter st section.

GARLAND **DOG** COLLAR

LEVEL
Intermediate

SIZES
The finished collar cover measures approximately 1¹/₂in/4cm wide for all sizes, and the lengths are as follows:
Extra-extra small—to fit collar size 10in/25cm
Extra-small—to fit collar size 12in/30.5cm
Small—to fit collar size 14in/35.5cm
Medium—to fit collar size 16in/40.5cm
Large—to fit collar size 18in/45.5cm
Extra-large—to fit collar size 20in/50.5cm

MATERIALS
Fingering/Super Fine Weight Yarn (CYCA 1) approx. 200 yds in main color
MC mustard (shown in *Jaeger Matchmaker Merino 4-Ply*)
Approx. 200 yds of same yarn, each in 6 different colors:
A (purple), **B** (maroon), **C** (blue-green), **D** (rust), **E** (lavender), and **F** (green), OR any scraps of leftover fine-weight yarn at hand (shown in *Rowan Scottish Tweed 4-Ply*)
Pair of size 3 (3.25mm) knitting needles

GAUGE
28 sts and 36 rows to 4in/10cm measured over St st using size 3 (3.25mm) needles and MC.

ABBREVIATIONS
See page 31.

TO MAKE COLLAR COVER
With size 3 (3.25mm) needles and MC, cast on 24 sts.
Work 2 rows in garter st (knit every row).
Beg with a k row, work in St st until collar cover measures 9 (11: 13: 15: 17: 19)in/ 22.5 (28: 33: 38: 43: 48)cm from cast-on edge, ending with a p row.
Work 2 rows in garter st, ending with a WS row.
Next row (RS) Bind off first 12 sts knitwise, k to end. *(12 sts.)*
Work 10 rows in garter st.
Bind off knitwise.

FLOWER 1
With size 3 (3.25mm) needles and A, cast on 40 sts.
Knit 1 row.

First petal
Next row (RS) K10, then turn, leaving rem sts unworked.
Working on these 10 sts only, make first petal as follows:
Purl 1 row.
Cont in St st throughout, inc 1 st at each end of next row and at each end of foll alt row, ending with a k row. *(14 sts.)*

Purl 1 row.
Dec 1 st at each end of next row and at each end of every foll alt row until 2 sts rem, ending with a k row.
Next row (WS) P2tog, then break off yarn, thread tail end through rem st, and pull tight to fasten off.

Second petal
With RS facing, return to sts left unworked and using D, k10, then turn, leaving rem sts unworked.
Working on these 10 sts only, make second petal as follows:

24

Knit 1 row.
Cont in garter st throughout, inc 1 st at each end of next row and at each end of foll alt row. *(14 sts.)*
Knit 1 row.
Dec 1 st at each end of next row and at each end of every foll alt row until 2 sts rem.
Next row K2tog, then break off yarn, thread tail end through rem st, and pull tight to fasten off.

Third and fourth petals
Cont as set, working third petal in St st in A as for first petal, and fourth (final) petal in garter st in D as for second petal.

FLOWER 2
With size 3 (3.25mm) needles and C, cast on 32 sts.
Knit 1 row.

First petal
Next row (RS) K10, then turn, leaving rem sts unworked.
Working on these 10 sts only, make first petal as follows:
Cont in garter st throughout, inc 1 st at each end of next row and at each end of foll alt row. *(14 sts.)*
Dec 1 st at each end of next row and at each end of every foll alt row until 2 sts rem.
Next row K2tog, then break off yarn, thread tail end through rem st, and pull tight to fasten off.

Second petal
With RS facing, return to sts left unworked and using D, k6, then turn, leaving rem sts unworked.
Working on these 6 sts only, make second petal as follows:
Purl 1 row.
Cont in St st throughout, inc 1 st at each end of next row and at each end of 2 foll alt rows, ending with a k row. *(12 sts.)*

Purl 1 row.
Work 2 rows in St st, ending with a p row.
Dec 1 st at each end of next row and at each end of every foll alt row until 2 sts rem, ending with a k row.
Next row (WS) P2tog, then break off yarn, thread tail end through rem st, and pull tight to fasten off.

Third and fourth petals
Cont as set, working third petal in garter st in C across 10 sts as for first petal, and fourth (final) petal in St st in D across 6 sts as for second petal.

STAMENS (MAKE 6)
With size 3 (3.25mm) needles and E, cast on 14 sts.
Bind off knitwise.
Make 5 more stamens in same way.
(If you want stamens to look particularly botanical, sew over and over end of each stamen to make the stigma, using F.)

LEAVES (MAKE 3)
With size 3 (3.25mm) needles and F, cast on 5 sts.
1st row (RS) *K1, k into front and back of next st—called *inc into next st*; rep from * once more, k1. *(7 sts.)*
2nd row and all foll WS rows Purl to end.
3rd row K2, inc into next st, k1, inc into next st, k2. *(9 sts.)*
5th row K3, inc into next st, k1, inc into next st, k3. *(11 sts.)*
7th row K4, inc into next st, k1, inc into next st, k4. *(13 sts.)*
9th row K5, inc into next st, k1 inc into next st, k5. *(15 sts.)*
11th row K to end.
13th row K1, k2tog, k9, k2tog, k1. *(13 sts.)*
15th row K1, k2tog, k7, k2tog, k1. *(11 sts.)*
17th row K1, k2tog, k5, k2tog, k1. *(9 sts.)*

19th row K1, k2tog, k3, k2tog, k1. *(7 sts.)*
21st row K1, k2tog, k1, k2tog, k1. *(5 sts.)*
Bind off purlwise.

PETALS (MAKE 2)
With size 3 (3.25mm) needles and B, cast on 4 sts.
Working in garter st throughout, inc 1 st at each end of first row and at each end of 3 foll alt rows. *(12 sts.)*
Knit 1 row.
Dec 1 st at each end of next row and at each end of 4 foll alt rows. *(2 sts.)*
Knit 1 row.
Next row (RS) K2tog, then break off yarn, thread tail end through rem st, and pull tight to fasten off.
Make second petal in same way.

TO FINISH
Press collar cover, leaves, and petals lightly on wrong side, following instructions on yarn label.
Fold collar cover in half lengthwise with right sides together and sew long side edges together to form a tube. Turn right side out and press again.

Add petals and leaves
Curl flower 1 around on itself and sew together at base so that it forms a four-petaled flower. Sew three stamens to center of flower.
Sew flower 2 together in same way.
Arrange flowers, leaves, and petals at center of collar as shown, positioning bound-off end of leaves and cast-on end of petals under flowers. Sew in place as arranged.
Sew bound-off edge of collar cover to corresponding section of cast-on edge.
Slip cover onto dog's collar, positioning buckle over garter st section.

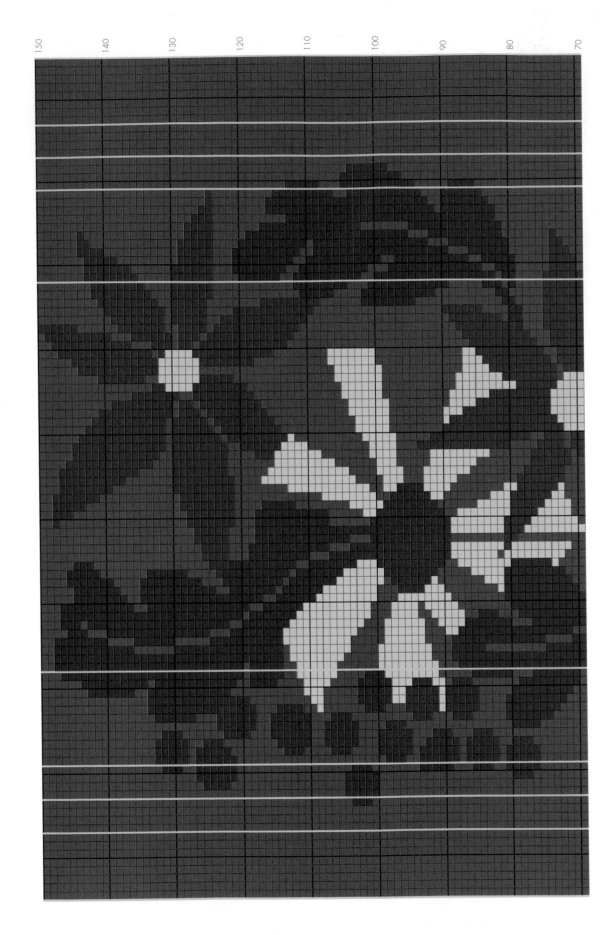

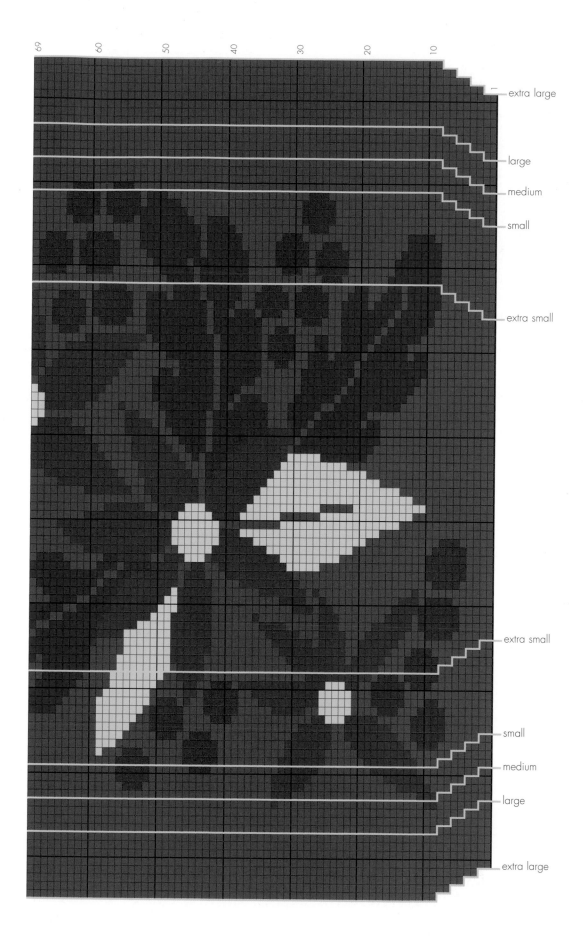

extra large

large

medium

small

extra small

extra small

small

medium

large

extra large

Spot **Dog** Coat Chart (page 10)

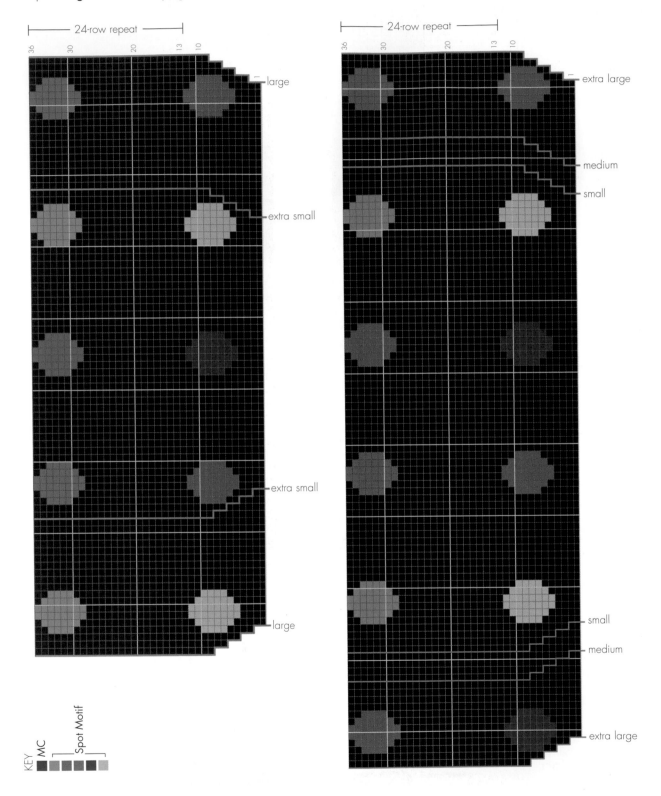

Spot **Dog**
Collar Chart
(page 21)

KEY
☐ MC
■ Spot Motif

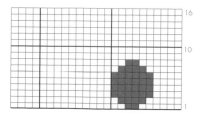

Hell's Angel **Dog**
Collar Chart (page 22)

KEY
■ MC
■ A
☐ B
■ C

Floral **Dog**
Collar Chart
(page 20)

KEY
■ MC
■ A
■ B
■ C
■ D

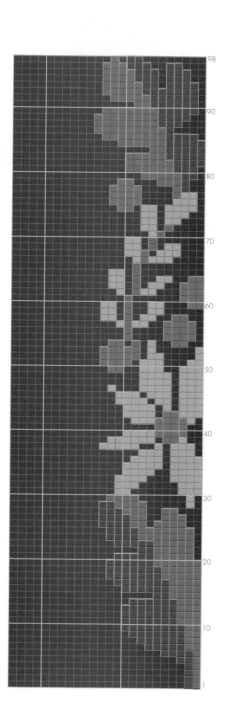

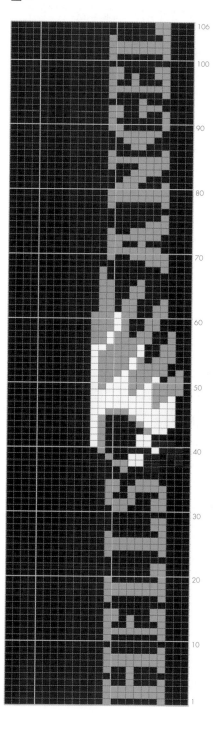

Soccer **Dog** Coat—
Number Chart (page 5)

Soccer **Dog** Coat—
Badge Chart (page 6)

KEY
■ MC
□ A

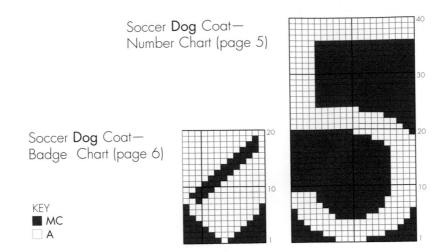

ABBREVIATIONS

The following are the abbreviations used in this book. Special abbreviations are given with individual patterns.

alt — alternate
beg — begin(ning)
cm — centimeter(s)
cont — continu(e)(ing)
dec — decreas(e)(ing)
DK — double knitting (a lightweight yarn)
foll — follow(s)(ing)
g — gram(s)
in — inch(es)
inc — increas(e)(ing)
k — knit
k2tog — knit next 2 sts together
m — meter(s)
MC — main color (of yarn)
mm — millimeter(s)
oz — ounce(s)
p — purl
p2tog — purl next 2 sts together
patt — pattern

psso — pass slipped stitch over
rem — remain(s)(ing)
rep — repeat(s)(ing)
rev St st — reverse stockinette stitch; purl sts on RS rows and knit sts on WS rows
RS — right side
sl — slip
st(s) — stitch(es)
St st — stockinette stitch; knit sts on RS rows and purl sts on WS rows
tbl — through back loop(s)
tog — together
WS — wrong side
yo — yarn over (yarn over right-hand needle to make a new stitch)

* — Repeat instructions after asterisk or between asterisks as many times as instructed.
[ ] — Repeat instructions inside square brackets as many times as instructed
- — Where a hyphen appears instead of a number, it means that instructions do not apply to that size

STANDARD YARN WEIGHT CHART

Yarn Weight Symbol and Category Name	Super Fine 1	Fine 2	Light 3	Medium 4	Bulky 5	Super Bulky 6
Types of yarn in category	Sock, fingering, baby	Sport, baby	DK, light worsted	Worsted, afghan, Aran	Chunky, craft, rug	Bulky, roving
Knit gauge range in St st in 4 in.*	27–32 sts	23–26 sts	21–24 sts	16–20 sts	12–15 sts	6–11 sts
Recommended metric needle size	2.25–3.25 mm	3.25–3.75 mm	3.75–4.5 mm	4.5–5.5 mm	5.5–8 mm	8 mm and larger
Recommended U.S. needle size	1–3	3–5	5–7	7–9	9–11	11 and larger
Crochet gauge range in sc in 4 in.*	21–31 sts	16–20 sts	12–17 sts	11–14 sts	8–11 sts	5–9 sts
Recommended metric hook size	2.25–3.5 mm	3.5–4.5 mm	4.5–5.5 mm	5.5–6.5 mm	6.5–9 mm	9 mm and larger
Recommended U.S. hook size	B/1–E/4	E/4–7	7–I/9	I/9–K/10.5	K/10.5–M/13	M/13 and larger

*The information in this table reflects the most commonly used gauges and needle or hook sizes for the specific yarn categories.

YARN SPECIFICS

The accessories in this book have been designed using Rowan and Jaeger Yarns, which are widely available throughout the United States, Europe, and over the Internet. Visit www.knitrowan.com where you will find a full range of yarns, colors, and suppliers. If you are a beginner, you can go to a local yarn store where the helpful staff will give you all the assistance you need to track down yarns.

The majority of these pet accessories are knitted in double-knitting-weight wool yarns. If you decide to use a yarn other than the specified yarn, do remember to knit a 4in (10cm) square to check the gauge and then adjust the needle size accordingly.

The number of yards (meters) per $1^3/_4$oz (50g) ball varies from yarn to yarn, so when using a substitute yarn, be sure to calculate the number of balls you need by the number of yards (meters) rather than by weight.

Some of the designs use small amounts of several colors. These give you the opportunity to use up leftover yarns. Before beginning, however, check the yarn descriptions to make sure that your leftovers are a good match in thickness to the main color you are using.

GAUGE

Working your knitting to the correct size can be important, especially for dog coats, so be sure to knit a gauge swatch. Count the number of stitches and rows to 4in (10cm) on your swatch. If your swatch has more rows or stitches than the number specified, then use knitting needles that are one size larger, and if it has fewer stitches or rows, then try one size smaller needles. Getting the number of stitches to 4in (10cm) right is more important than the number of rows, as length is generally determined by merely knitting to a specified length in inches (centimeters).

Working a gauge swatch sounds tedious, but it is definitely worth the time it takes, particularly if the design comes in various sizes. The swatch also gives you a chance to see how the yarn and stitch pattern knit up. Keep these swatches, and once you have collected about 20, sew them together into a blanket for your pet.

DOG COAT SIZES

The dog coat patterns are written for five sizes. But dogs do vary enormously in size. Here are the measurements on which we based most of our dog coats:

	Chest	Body length	Collar
Extra small	12in/30.5cm	12in/30.5cm	10in/25.5cm
Small	16in/40.5cm	14in/35.5cm	11in/27.5cm
Medium	20in/50.5cm	18in/45.5cm	13in/33cm
Large	24in/61cm	22in/56cm	15in/38cm
Extra large	26in/66cm	24in/61cm	17in/43cm

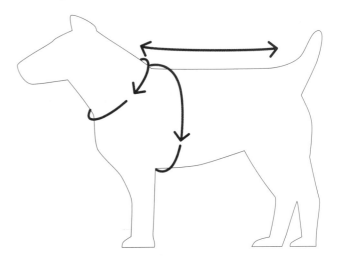

When you are measuring your dog to decide which size to knit, the most important measurement is around the widest part of the dog's chest, just behind the front legs, followed by the collar size and then the body length. For example, if your dog has a medium-sized rib cage, a small neck, and a long back, it is best to opt for Medium.

It is very easy to shorten or lengthen a dog coat, and the best place is mentioned in the individual patterns.

PROTECT YOUR PETS

The most essential thing to remember when knitting for your pets is to make sure that all beads and buttons are securely sewn on—you don't want your animals to swallow them.